God's Q
Crafting Your Story
In
Divine Harmony

Reflections On The Life Of The Apostle Paul
Personal Applications
Prayer Focus
Summaries
Key Takeaways
Ideal For Personal or Group Study

God's Quill: Crafting Your Story In Divine Harmony
© 2024 David Griggs

All rights reserved. No part of this publication may be reproduced, distributed, or transmitted in any form or by any means, including photocopying, recording, or other electronic or mechanical methods, without the prior written permission of the author, except in the case of brief quotations embodied in critical reviews and certain other non-commercial uses permitted by copyright law. For permission requests, please contact the author at gdaved@gmail.com.

This book has been thoughtfully designed for self-reflection and personal spiritual growth. The content is intended to guide readers toward a deeper understanding of how their life's story is being crafted by God, recognizing that every chapter holds purpose and meaning.

This material is for individual use only and is not intended for commercial sale or mass distribution without the express written consent of the author.

Table of Contents

God's Quill Crafting Your Story In Divine Harmony	1
Introduction	6
Chapter One	11
Chapter Two	14
Chapter Three	18
Chapter Four	23
Chapter Five	30
Chapter Six	34
Chapter Seven	38
Chapter Eight	42
Chapter Nine	47
Chapter Ten	52
Chapter Eleven	57
Chapter Twelve	62
Chapter Thirteen	67
Chapter Fourteen	71
Author's Page	75

Prologue
Saul of Tarsus: A Story of Transformation and Surrender
Introduction

Saul of Tarsus, later known as the Apostle Paul, stands as one of the most influential figures in early Christianity. His life journey, marked by fervent zeal and a dramatic transformation, illustrates how God can radically reshape a life for His purposes. Saul's beginnings were steeped in religious tradition and commitment, but his journey would ultimately take a remarkable turn, proving that God can rewrite any story.

Born in Tarsus, a major city in the Roman province of Cilicia, Saul was raised in a devout Jewish family that adhered strictly to Pharisaic traditions. From a young age, Saul was immersed in Jewish law and customs, and this foundation became a significant part of his identity. His formal education began under the renowned rabbi Gamaliel, one of the foremost teachers of Jewish law at the time. Saul's rigorous education under Gamaliel deeply ingrained in him a strong adherence to the law and molded him into a "Pharisee of Pharisees," as he later described himself (Philippians 3:5). Saul was zealous for the traditions of his ancestors, and this zeal shaped his worldview.

However, Saul's fervent commitment to Judaism and the Pharisaic traditions fueled an intense hostility toward the emerging Christian movement. To Saul, Jesus' followers were a threat to the purity of Jewish law, a sect that needed to be eradicated. This passion led Saul to become a fierce persecutor of the early Christian church, driven by a conviction that he was protecting his faith.

Saul's Role as a Persecutor

One of the pivotal moments in Saul's life as a persecutor came during the stoning of Stephen, the first Christian martyr. Stephen, a deacon in the early church, was brought before the Sanhedrin on charges of blasphemy and condemned to death. Saul was present at the execution, and while he did not cast stones, he approved of the act by guarding the clothes of those who did (Acts 7:58). This moment highlighted Saul's role as a willing participant in the persecution of Christians, setting him on a path to become one of the most feared figures among the early believers.

Following the stoning of Stephen, Saul's mission to eradicate the Christian movement intensified. He went from house to house, dragging both men and women from their homes and imprisoning them (Acts 8:3). His actions caused many Christians to flee Jerusalem, which paradoxically resulted in the gospel being spread further. Saul was relentless, obtaining letters from the high priest that authorized him to arrest any followers of "the Way" in Damascus and bring them back to Jerusalem in chains. Saul's zeal knew no bounds, and he was determined to stamp out this movement.

A Dramatic Encounter on the Road to Damascus

Little did Saul know that his journey to Damascus would change his life forever. As Saul traveled along the road to Damascus, a bright light suddenly flashed around him, and he fell to the ground. He heard a voice say, "Saul, Saul, why are you persecuting Me?" (Acts 9:4). Blinded and confused, Saul asked, "Who are You, Lord?" The voice replied, "I am Jesus, whom you are persecuting" (Acts 9:5). This encounter with the risen Christ was the turning point in Saul's life. Struck blind, he was led into Damascus, where he waited for three days, fasting and praying.

This dramatic encounter was more than just a moment of personal transformation—it was the moment when God's quill began rewriting Saul's story. The persecutor of Christians was now being called to be one of the faith's greatest apostles. Saul's transformation into Paul was a profound testament to the power of God's grace and His ability to redeem even the darkest paths.

GOD'S QUILL: TRANSFORMING Lives

Saul's story is not just about personal redemption; it is a powerful reminder that God is the ultimate author of our lives. His transformation from a zealous persecutor to an ardent apostle illustrates that God can take even the most broken, misguided lives and rewrite them for His glory. Just as Saul became Paul, the one who spread the gospel to the Gentiles, so too can our lives be transformed when we surrender to God's plan.

This narrative challenges us to reflect on our own stories. Are we allowing God to hold the pen, or are we trying to write our own narratives? Paul's journey shows us that God can take control of our lives in ways we could never imagine. No one is beyond the reach of God's grace. Paul's dramatic transformation teaches us that even when we are on a path far from God's will, He can intervene, turn our hearts toward Him, and give our lives new purpose.

Reflection Questions

1. **Trusting God's Control**: Are there areas of your life where you are struggling to let go and let God take control? How might surrendering those areas to God bring about transformation?
2. **Experiencing Transformation**: Reflect on how God has already worked in your life. What moments stand out where God's intervention changed your path?
3. **God's Greater Plan**: How does Saul's transformation into Paul encourage you to trust that God has a greater plan for your life, even when things seem uncertain or difficult?
4. **Surrendering the Pen**: Are you willing to let God be the author of your story, even if it means unexpected changes or challenges along the way?

Embracing God's Narrative

Today, many of us face uncertainties, challenges, and moments of doubt. We wonder if our lives have a purpose or if we've strayed too far from God's plan. Like Saul, we may feel that our past mistakes or current struggles disqualify us from being used by God. But Saul's journey to becoming Paul shows us that no one is beyond God's reach. The key is surrendering our lives to God's authorship. In a world where we often strive to control every aspect of our existence, this story invites us to relinquish control, trusting that God's plan is far more profound than we could ever imagine.

Prayer Focus

- **A Willing Heart**: Pray for the courage to surrender your life to God's authorship. Ask Him to guide you through both the known and the unknown parts of your journey.
- **Transformation**: Pray for God's transforming power to work in your heart, just as He worked in Saul's. Ask for His grace to turn your mistakes, challenges, and uncertainties into opportunities for growth and purpose.
- **Trust in His Plan**: Pray for the faith to trust in God's greater plan for your life, even when it takes unexpected turns.

Summary

Saul of Tarsus began his journey as a zealous Pharisee, committed to preserving Jewish law by persecuting the early Christian church. His passion to eradicate the followers of "the Way" led him to witness the stoning of Stephen and embark on a mission to imprison believers. Yet, on the road to Damascus, Saul's life took a radical turn when he encountered the risen Christ. From that moment, Saul's story was rewritten by the hand of God, transforming him into the Apostle Paul, one of the most influential figures in the spread of the gospel.

Key Takeaways

1. **God's Transformative Power**: No one is beyond God's reach. Saul's dramatic conversion shows that even the most fervent opposition to God can be transformed into passionate devotion.
2. **Surrendering to God's Plan**: When we surrender control of

our lives to God, He can take even our darkest moments and rewrite them into stories of grace and redemption.
3. **Living as God's Masterpiece**: Our lives are not a series of random events but chapters in a greater narrative written by God. When we allow Him to be the author, our stories become masterpieces of His grace.
4. **The Power of Redemption**: Paul's story reminds us that our past, no matter how misguided, can be redeemed and used for God's glory.

Introduction

The Pen in God's Hand
A Study of Paul's Transformed Narrative

Purpose of the Series:
This series, *God's Quill: The Pen in God's Hands,* focuses on how God, as the ultimate author, reshapes and redirects lives according to His divine purpose. Through the life of the Apostle Paul, we explore how God rewrites our stories, using Paul's background, conversion, missionary journeys, and letters to reveal how God's hand was active in every chapter of his life. Much like Paul, our lives are subject to God's authorship when we surrender to His will.

Paul's Life as God's Narrative

Paul's journey stands as one of the most profound examples of transformation in Scripture. More than just a personal shift from being a persecutor of Christians to becoming a devoted apostle, his story illustrates the power of God's divine authorship.

Paul (originally Saul) was deeply rooted in Jewish tradition, raised as a Pharisee, with an intense devotion to the law. His early life and upbringing shaped him into a zealous defender of his faith, leading him to violently oppose the Christian movement. Yet, God's plan for Saul was greater than his earthly ambitions.

On the road to Damascus, God intervened. In one divine moment, Saul's path was forever changed. This encounter with the risen Christ transformed Saul into Paul, the great apostle. Paul's life, once driven by his own determination, was now being rewritten by God's grace. He became a champion for the gospel, planting churches, mentoring believers, and writing letters that form a significant part of the New Testament. This transformation teaches us that no life is beyond the reach of God's redemptive hand.

Trusting God's Greater Plan

In today's world, we are often encouraged to meticulously plan our lives—careers, relationships, and personal goals. But, as Paul's story shows, God's plans for us often differ from our own. Sometimes, we find ourselves on unexpected paths, facing circumstances we didn't foresee. Yet, we can trust that God, as the divine author, is weaving each chapter of our lives with purpose.

Surrendering to His will means trusting Him with both the known and the unknown, believing that His narrative for our lives is far greater than anything we could write for ourselves. When we relinquish control, we allow God to use our experiences—both triumphs and failures—to shape us for His glory and to impact the lives of others.

The Call to Surrender Control

Paul's story highlights the need to surrender control and allow God to guide our lives. Before his conversion, Saul pursued a path of self-determined righteousness. His zeal for the law led him to persecute Christians in an effort to preserve his own vision of religious purity. But once Saul encountered Christ, he was forced to give up control. The pen of his life was handed over to God, who began rewriting his purpose. His new identity as Paul, the apostle, was rooted in grace, not self-righteousness. He was now driven by Christ's mission to spread the gospel to the world.

Like Paul, we are called to surrender our lives to God's authorship. While we may not experience a dramatic conversion like Paul's, God still speaks to us through His Word, prayer, and our circumstances. When we stop trying to control every detail and instead trust God with the narrative, we open ourselves to His divine plan—one that leads to purpose and fulfillment beyond what we could imagine.

REFLECTION QUESTIONS

1. **God as the Author of Your Life:** How do you feel about the idea of God being the author of your life story? Does it bring you peace to know He is in control, or is it challenging to surrender your plans to Him?
2. **Surrendering Control:** Are there specific areas of your life—career, relationships, future plans—where you find it difficult to surrender control? What steps can you take to fully entrust those areas to God?
3. **Paul's Transformation as an Encouragement:** Consider how Paul's transformation from persecutor to apostle can encourage you to view your own challenges, mistakes, or unexpected changes as part of God's greater narrative. How might your past, when surrendered to God, be rewritten into a story of redemption and purpose?
4. **Viewing Challenges as Part of God's Plan:** In what ways do the hardships and uncertainties in your life feel like obstacles to your plans? How might viewing them as chapters in God's larger story change your perspective?

Prayer Focus

- **Pray for an Open Heart:** Ask God to help you be open to His leading. Pray for the courage to let go of control, to lay down your plans, and to trust in His greater vision for your life.
- **Seek God's Clarity:** Ask for insight to recognize where God is actively working in your life, especially in areas where you feel uncertain or challenged. Pray for discernment to see how He is shaping your story, even in moments that seem like detours.
- **Embrace Transformation:** Pray for a heart willing to be transformed like Paul. Ask God to use both your strengths and

weaknesses, your past mistakes and triumphs, to reflect His glory and purpose.

Summary and Key Takeaways

- **Key Takeaway 1:** God is the ultimate author of our lives. Just as He rewrote Paul's story, He is actively shaping each of our lives in ways that exceed our own plans and expectations.
- **Key Takeaway 2:** Surrendering control of our story to God leads to a life of deeper purpose, fulfillment, and peace. When we trust Him with our future, we allow Him to work through us in ways we couldn't foresee.
- **Key Takeaway 3:** Paul's transformation from persecutor to apostle teaches us that no one is beyond the reach of God's grace. When we surrender our lives to Him, He can rewrite even the most broken stories into powerful testimonies of redemption.

Actionable Steps

In today's world, we are often encouraged to plan every detail of our lives. But, as Paul's story reminds us, God's plan often leads us down unexpected paths. Here are a few steps you can take to surrender your story to God:

- **Pray for Guidance:** Start by asking God to reveal where He is at work in your life. Pray for wisdom and discernment to recognize His leading.
- **Release Control:** Identify the areas of your life where you are holding too tightly to your own plans. Pray for the courage to let go and trust God's guidance.
- **Reflect on Your Journey:** Take time to reflect on how God has already worked in your life. Consider the moments when His

plan differed from yours, and how those moments have shaped you.

FINAL THOUGHTS

Paul's life story is a powerful example of how God can transform any life, no matter how far off course it seems. By trusting in His divine authorship, we can live with the confidence that He is shaping us for a greater purpose. As you study Paul's life, consider how God may be rewriting your own story, inviting you to surrender control and follow His perfect plan.

Chapter One

Beginning The Journey
The Starting Point

Every story has a starting point, a beginning where the divine threads start to weave the narrative of a life. For Saul, later to be named Paul, this beginning is rooted just north of the Mediterranean Sea, in the ancient city of Tarsus of Cilicia, located in what is now modern-day Turkey.

Tarsus was a city rich in culture and history, a hub of commerce and learning in the ancient world. It was here, amidst the bustling streets and vibrant marketplaces, that Saul's early life unfolded. His upbringing was steeped in both the Jewish traditions of his family and the Hellenistic influences of his surroundings. This unique blend of cultures and philosophies would later play a significant role in shaping his approach to spreading the gospel.

Though retaining his Jewish birthright, Paul was a Roman citizen from birth. As a Roman citizen, this afforded him significant rights and privileges. These included the right to a fair trial, protection against certain forms of punishment such as scourging, and the right to appeal directly to the Emperor in Rome. These legal protections provided Paul with opportunities to further his missionary work and defend himself against accusations, regardless of where he was in the Roman Empire.

Caesar Augustus had permitted Jews in Tarsus to become Roman citizens, an uncommon privilege for a Jew. This citizenship would grant Paul unique opportunities and protections that would prove crucial in his later missions. When arrested in Jerusalem and sentenced to be whipped and scourged by the Romans soldiers, Paul asked the centurion: "Is it lawful for you to whip a man who is a Roman, and uncondemned ... The centurion said to Paul, 'With a large sum I obtained this citizenship.' Paul replied, 'But I was born a citizen.'" (Acts 22:25,28).

When arrested in Phillipi, a Roman colony, Paul and Silas were whipped and thrown into jail overnight. We find them worshipping God at midnight and bringing a jailor and his family to saving faith in Christ. In the morning, the jailers wished to release these two men quietly and ordered them to leave the city, but Paul refused.

"They have beaten us openly, uncondemned Romans and thrown us into prison ... The officers and magistrates were afraid when they heard they were Romans" (Acts 16:37-38).

The Bible is clear that we have dual citizenship and with it all the rights and privileges afforded to its citizens.

First of all is our heavenly citizenship

"For our citizenship is in heaven and from it we eagerly wait for the Savior, the Lord Jesus Christ" (Philippians 3:20).

"But now they desire a better, that is, a heavenly country. Therefore God is not ashamed to be called their God, for He has prepared a city for them" (Hebrews 11:16).

Secondly is our earthly citizenship

"Let every soul be subject to the governing authorities. For there is no authority except from God and the authorities that exist are appointed by God ... Render therefore to all their due: taxes to whom taxes are due, customs to whom customs are due, fear to whom fear, honor to whom honor" (Romans 13:1-7).

Until the day of our homecoming, we continue to exercise our rights as citizens in our respective countries. As with Paul, we use our rights to advance the gospel of Jesus Christ.

Modern Application:

The story of Paul's transformation from a persecutor to an apostle reminds us that God is the ultimate author of our lives. Just as He rewrote Paul's life, He is at work in ours, orchestrating events and leading us through both trials and triumphs. Often, we try to control our own narratives, but surrendering the pen to God allows Him to turn even our darkest chapters into stories of redemption and purpose.

Many of us face challenges, uncertainties, and doubts about the direction of our lives. We wonder if we're on the right path or if we've made too many mistakes for God to use us. Paul's life is a powerful testimony that God can transform anyone's story, no matter how far they've strayed. The question is whether we will allow God to take control and write the next chapter.

Reflection Questions:

- How do you feel about God being the author of your life story?
- Are there areas of your life where you need to surrender control to God?

Prayer Focus:

- Pray for an open heart to allow God to guide the narrative of your life.
- Ask for wisdom and discernment to recognize His hand in your daily decisions and challenges.

Summary and Key Takeaways:

- Key Takeaway 1: God is the ultimate author of our lives, and His plans for us are greater than our own.
- Key Takeaway 2: Surrendering control to God allows Him to turn even our struggles into opportunities for growth and redemption.

Chapter Two

Saul's Bar Mitzvah Ceremony
Tarsus of Cilicia

In the bustling city of Tarsus, nestled in the region of Cilicia, a significant rite of passage unfolded for a young boy named Saul. At the tender age of 13, Saul was about to become a "son of the commandment" through the sacred ceremony of his Bar Mitzvah. This milestone marked his transition into religious adulthood, where he would now be responsible for observing the commandments of the Torah.

The preparations for Saul's Bar Mitzvah began months in advance. His parents, devout Jews, were deeply involved in the process. His father, a respected tent maker, ensured that Saul was well-versed in the Torah, guiding him through its intricate laws and teachings. His mother, known for her piety and wisdom, provided emotional support and nurtured his spiritual growth. Together, they fostered an environment of faith and learning, preparing Saul for this momentous day.

The ceremony took place in the local synagogue, a cornerstone of the Jewish community in Tarsus. The synagogue itself was a modest yet dignified structure, with its walls adorned with religious symbols and scriptures. The rabbi, a venerable figure who had known Saul since his birth, played a crucial role. In the days leading up to the Bar Mitzvah, the rabbi offered intensive instruction, helping Saul perfect his Torah reading and understand the deeper meanings behind the sacred texts. The synagogue buzzed with excitement as friends and family gathered to witness Saul's transition.

GOD'S QUILL CRAFTING YOUR STORY IN DIVINE HARMONY

On the day of the ceremony, Saul donned a traditional tallit, its fringes symbolizing the commandments he was now bound to follow. The congregation rose as he ascended the bimah, the elevated platform where he would read from the Torah. With a mix of nerves and pride, Saul chanted the Torah portion he had diligently practiced. His clear, youthful voice resonated through the synagogue, capturing the attention and admiration of all present.

After the Torah reading, Saul delivered a heartfelt d'var Torah, a brief sermon reflecting on the passage he had read. He spoke with wisdom beyond his years, sharing insights that touched the hearts of his listeners. The rabbi, beaming with pride, blessed Saul, acknowledging his new status as a full member of the Jewish community.

The celebration that followed was joyous and lively. Saul's parents hosted a festive meal, where family and friends gathered to honor the young Bar Mitzvah boy. Traditional songs and dances filled the air, and blessings were showered upon Saul. Gifts were presented, many of which were books and religious items to support his continued spiritual journey.

The feast was a rich display of local and traditional Jewish cuisine, including dishes like stuffed grape leaves, honey cakes, and savory stews. The aroma of freshly baked challah bread mingled with the scent of spiced wine, creating an atmosphere of warmth and festivity.

Saul's Bar Mitzvah in Tarsus was more than a ceremony; it was a testament to the enduring faith and traditions of the Jewish people. It marked the beginning of Saul's lifelong commitment to his heritage, a commitment that would eventually lead him to become one of the most influential figures in religious history. As the celebrations continued into the evening, the sense of community and shared heritage was palpable, leaving an indelible mark on young Saul's heart and soul.

Modern Application:

Today, Saul's Bar Mitzvah serves as a reminder of the importance of marking significant spiritual milestones in our own lives. Just as Saul was shaped by the teachings of his faith community, we, too, are called to immerse ourselves in spiritual growth and to celebrate the moments when we step deeper into God's plan for us. Whether it's through baptism, confirmation, or other personal commitments, these ceremonies and traditions help us acknowledge our role in God's unfolding narrative.

Reflection:

- What are the significant spiritual milestones in your life? How have they shaped your journey with God?
- How can you foster an environment of faith, learning, and spiritual growth in your own life or the lives of those around you?
- In what ways do you feel called to take on more responsibility in your spiritual walk, much like Saul did in his Bar Mitzvah?

Prayer Focus:

- **Pray for spiritual growth and maturity:** Ask God to help you grow in faith and understanding, much like Saul's parents prepared him for his Bar Mitzvah.
- **Ask for guidance:** Pray for God's direction as you step into new phases of your spiritual journey, surrendering your plans to His divine authorship.

Summary and Key Takeaways:

- **Key Takeaway 1:** Saul's Bar Mitzvah marked a key transition in his spiritual life, symbolizing the importance of stepping into responsibility and commitment in our relationship with God.
- **Key Takeaway 2:** Our spiritual journeys, like Saul's, are shaped by the traditions, teachings, and milestones that anchor us in

faith. These moments remind us of our place in God's greater narrative.
- **Key Takeaway 3:** Just as Saul was prepared for his future by his family and community, we are called to create environments that nurture spiritual growth and responsibility in ourselves and others.

The story of Saul's Bar Mitzvah reflects a life deeply rooted in faith and tradition, but also open to the transformative power of God. It was the first step in a journey that would ultimately lead Saul to become Paul, an apostle who helped shape the foundation of the Christian church. As we reflect on his story, may we be encouraged to take on the responsibilities of faith in our own lives and trust that God is writing a beautiful and purposeful narrative for each of us.

Chapter Three

Learning the Trade
Tent Making and Spiritual Preparation
The Importance Of Teaching Our Children Well

In Jewish tradition, fathers taught their sons a trade to ensure they could provide for themselves and their families. This practice emphasized the importance of work and self-sufficiency. The Talmud, a central text of Rabbinic Judaism, states that a father who doesn't teach his son a trade teaches him to steal (Kiddushin 29a). Fathers usually passed down their own trade to their sons, giving hands-on training and apprenticeships from an early age. This method made sure skills were learned well and kept within the family.

Paul's father might have belonged to a guild of craftsmen who oversaw tent making in Tarsus. Unlike today's canvas tents, the materials used were commonly found in Tarsus and the surrounding region.

Tent Making Material

The most common material was goat hair, especially for larger and more durable tents. Goat hair was spun into a coarse fabric that was water-resistant and great for outdoor use.

Leather from tanned animal skins made tents more durable and weather-resistant or was used for specific parts of the tent, like reinforcements and fastenings.

Linen was also used for lighter, more portable tents, but it was less common due to its cost and being less durable compared to goat hair and leather.

Using His Skills For Ministry

GOD'S QUILL CRAFTING YOUR STORY IN DIVINE HARMONY

Paul's skill in tent making was crucial for his missionary work. It allowed him to support himself financially and not be a burden on the communities he served. Some key instances where Paul used his tent-making skills include:

- **Corinth:** In Acts 18:1-3, Paul stayed with Aquila and Priscilla, who were also tent makers. Paul worked with them while preaching in the local synagogue. This arrangement allowed Paul to finance his stay and mission in Corinth.
- **Ephesus:** Although not explicitly mentioned, Paul likely continued his tent-making trade while in Ephesus, as he spent a significant amount of time there (Acts 19:1-10). This would have supported him during his extensive missionary activities.
- **Thessalonica:** In 1 Thessalonians 2:9 and 2 Thessalonians 3:7-8, Paul mentions working "night and day" so as not to be a burden to the Thessalonians. While he does not specify tent making, it is reasonable to assume he used his trade to support himself.

Paul was committed to being self-sufficient and wanted to preach the gospel without relying on financial support from the communities he served. This practice also allowed him to connect with local craftsmen and workers, providing more opportunities for evangelism.

Before Paul became known for his missionary journeys and his letters that shaped early Christianity, he was Saul of Tarsus, a skilled tent maker. This trade, passed down from his father, may have seemed ordinary, but in God's hands, it became a tool for Paul's ministry. The simple work of stitching fabric together and creating shelter provided a means for him to support himself as he spread the Gospel across various regions, enabling him to serve without financial burden on the fledgling churches.

The physical act of making tents parallels the spiritual preparation God was performing in Paul's heart. As Paul worked diligently with his hands, God was molding his character, using every moment to shape him for the monumental task ahead. After Paul's dramatic encounter with Christ on the road to Damascus, he spent time in solitude in Arabia and Damascus. This often-overlooked period was essential for his spiritual formation. In the quiet and the stillness, Paul received revelations that would prepare him for his apostolic mission.

In Paul's life, we see how God uses both the ordinary (tent making) and the extraordinary (his dramatic conversion) to equip His servants. As Paul stitched together pieces of fabric, God was stitching together the fabric of his new identity, transforming him into a man who would change the course of history.

Tent Making and Spiritual Preparation

Paul's time of preparation wasn't just about learning a trade—it was about God shaping his heart and character. In our fast-paced society, it's easy to overlook the importance of spiritual formation. But just as Paul needed time in the desert to prepare for his mission, we need moments of solitude, prayer, and study to equip us for the work God has for us. These quiet times are where God refines us, teaching us patience, humility, and dependence on Him.

Our jobs, responsibilities, and daily tasks might seem mundane at times, but like Paul's tent making, they can be part of God's plan for something greater. Just as Paul used his trade to connect with others and further the Gospel, we can use our work—whether in an office, at home, or in ministry—as a way to reflect God's love and truth.

Tent making can symbolize any work or role that sustains us while also providing opportunities to live out our faith. Whether it's building relationships with coworkers, being an example of Christ-like character, or simply doing our best with integrity, our work has purpose beyond the paycheck. God uses both our work and the quiet moments of spiritual preparation to equip us for His calling.

In today's world, the idea of "tent making" can be expanded to include any work we do that sustains our lives while also providing opportunities to live out our faith. Whether you're in an office, running a household, or working in a service industry, your work has purpose. Just as Paul saw his trade as a way to connect with people and further the Gospel, we too can use our professions to influence and uplift those around us.

As we juggle our responsibilities, we can take inspiration from Paul's example. Our work and our spiritual growth are not separate paths but intertwined journeys. By embracing both, we allow God to mold us into the people He calls us to be, ready to serve Him in every aspect of our lives.

Reflection Questions:

- How does your current work or daily responsibilities connect with God's larger purpose for your life?
- Are there moments in your life that you see as "ordinary", but that God may be using to shape your spiritual journey?
- Have you experienced a season of waiting or preparation where God was working in your heart, even if you couldn't see it at the time?

Prayer Focus:

- Pray for clarity in how God wants to use your current work or role in His plan.
- Ask God to help you see your daily responsibilities as opportunities for ministry and service.
- Pray for patience during times of waiting or preparation, trusting that God is molding you for a greater purpose.

Summary and Key Takeaways:

- **Key Takeaway 1:** God uses both the ordinary and extraordinary moments in our lives to prepare us for His work.

- **Key Takeaway 2:** Our work and daily tasks are not separate from our spiritual journey but are intertwined with God's purpose for our lives

Paul's life serves as a reminder that God uses both the practical and spiritual aspects of our lives for His purpose. Whether through our work, spiritual preparation, or life's unexpected turns, God is always shaping us into the people He has called us to be. The challenge is to trust His authorship, even when the story takes unexpected twists and turns.

Chapter Four

Gamaliel
A Legacy of Wisdom, Leniency, and Influence

Saul left Tarsus of Cilicia, possibly in his later teens, to study in Jerusalem under the renown Gamaliel. This trip, which Saul likely undertook by boat, was not merely a physical voyage but a passage towards his future as one of the most influential figures in Christianity. Tarsus would gradually fade into the horizon as they sailed on the calm waters of the Mediterranean Sea.

The boat, possibly a modest merchant vessel, would cut through the gentle waves, its sails catching the Mediterranean breeze. Along the way, Saul might have seen other ships, both large and small, crossing the busy trade routes of the ancient world.

As the boat hugged the coastline, he would be treated to stunning views of rugged cliffs, serene beaches, and small coastal villages. The scent of saltwater mingled with the aromatic breezes carrying hints of pine and citrus groves. Passing by the island of Cyprus, he would catch glimpses of its mountainous terrain and lush landscapes. The journey offered Saul ample time to reflect on his ambitions and the life-changing studies ahead.

Arrival In Judea

Approaching the Judean coastline, the landscape shifted dramatically. The boat would likely dock at Caesarea, a bustling seaport built by Herod the Great. He would continue by land through the Judean hills. The road to Jerusalem would lead him through rolling hills dotted with olive trees, vineyards, and ancient villages. The air would be filled with the sounds of nature and the distant hum of human activity.

Arrival In Jerusalem

Can you imagine his excitement as he neared Jerusalem, with its towering walls and majestic temple, which stood as a beacon of religious and cultural significance? His heart would pulse with excitement, his steps quickened, especially when he caught sight of the temple gleaming in the sunlight.

Studying Under Gamaliel

Studying under Gamaliel would be the pinnacle of Saul's academic and spiritual aspirations. Gamaliel, renowned for his wisdom and leniency in interpreting the law, would provide a nurturing yet challenging environment for his students. Saul would join other eager minds in rigorous debates and in-depth study of the Torah. As he would later state, he excelled even beyond his classmates. Lessons in the Temple courts buzzed with the fervor of intellectual pursuit. Gamaliel's teaching style, characterized by deep respect for tradition combined with openness to diverse interpretations, would profoundly shape Saul's thinking and approach to the scriptures.

Shaped For God's Destiny

Under Gamaliel's mentorship, Saul developed a robust understanding of Jewish law and an appreciation for the complexities of theological discourse. This period of intense study and reflection would lay the foundational stones for his later work as an apostle, influencing his teachings and writings that would eventually shape Christian theology.

Saul's journey from Tarsus to Jerusalem was a voyage filled with scenic beauty, spiritual anticipation, and academic rigor. The experiences and knowledge gained during this formative period under Gamaliel's tutelage helped to shape Saul into Paul, the apostle who would leave an indelible mark on history.

GOD'S QUILL CRAFTING YOUR STORY IN DIVINE HARMONY

Gamaliel was a highly esteemed figure in Jewish history, is described by the historian Josephus as coming from a "very illustrious" family. He was the grandson of the great rabbi Hillel the Elder, who founded the most lenient version of Pharisaism. As Hillel's successor, Gamaliel led the Pharisaic movement, known for its lenient approach in Palestinian Judaism. This leniency made him popular among the people, amplifying his influence within the Sanhedrin, the highest Jewish council.

Rabbinic Literature honors Gamaliel with the title "the Elder," similar to his grandfather, and he was one of only seven men in history to receive the title Rabban ("our master") instead of the more common Rabbi ("my master"). Although all Pharisees were highly regarded, Gamaliel was particularly revered. Luke's description of him as "respected by all the people" (Acts 5:34) underscores his exceptional status. This respect and influence are why Paul proudly cites his study under Gamaliel as a key aspect of his Jewish heritage (Acts 22:3).

As the head of the Pharisaic movement, Gamaliel had significant sway over the masses. The Pharisees, known for their lenient judgments, contrasted sharply with the severity of the Sadducees. As a co-chair of the Sanhedrin alongside the High Priest, Gamaliel's emphasis on leniency often influenced the council's deliberations. His authority was so profound that his personal orders were executed without debate, as seen when he commanded the apostles be removed from the courtroom (Acts 5:34). His speech, often translated as "I advise you" (Acts 5:38), is better rendered as "I say to you" (NASB), reflecting a strong authoritative pronouncement rather than mere advice.

Gamaliel's intervention in Acts 5 is a prime example of his influence. By advocating for leniency, he effectively reduced the apostles' sentence from capital punishment to flogging (Acts 5:38-40). This shift demonstrated his ability to sway even the Sadducean members of the Sanhedrin, who were generally more severe.

Beyond Acts 5, Gamaliel's influence permeates other areas of the New Testament. He emphasized the importance of study and the teacher-student relationship. He reached out to Jews in the Diaspora, and was tolerant of Gentiles, a trait his pupils and descendants continued.

Gamaliel also valued the Greek language, declaring it the only language into which the Torah could be perfectly translated.

Understanding these aspects of Gamaliel's life helps us appreciate his profound impact on his most famous student, Paul of Tarsus. Like Gamaliel, Paul mentored younger students, reached out to Jews in the Diaspora, included Greeks in his mission, and utilized the Greek version of Scripture. Paul's relationship with Gamaliel is evident in his teachings and practices, showing how deeply he was influenced by his master.

Gamaliel's legacy extends beyond his immediate influence on the Pharisaic movement. His teachings and principles significantly shaped early Christianity through his student Paul. Gamaliel's emphasis on leniency, education, and cultural inclusivity left an indelible mark on Jewish and Christian traditions alike.

Gamaliel, a highly esteemed figure in Jewish history, comes from a lineage of great influence. The historian Josephus describes Gamaliel's family as "very illustrious" (The Life of Josephus, 190-191), and Gamaliel himself was the grandson of Hillel the Elder, a revered rabbi known for his lenient interpretation of Jewish law. As the successor of his grandfather, Gamaliel became the leader of the Pharisaic movement, which emphasized a more compassionate and lenient approach in Palestinian Judaism. This leniency made him a beloved figure among the people and amplified his authority within the Sanhedrin, the highest Jewish governing council.

As the head of the Pharisaic movement, Gamaliel wielded significant influence, especially because the Pharisees were known for their leniency in contrast to the more rigid Sadducees. As a co-chair of the Sanhedrin, alongside the High Priest, his emphasis on compassion shaped many of the council's decisions. His authority was so strong that his directives were often carried out without resistance, as seen when he ordered the apostles be removed from the courtroom (Acts 5:34). When he addressed the Sanhedrin, his words were not mere suggestions but authoritative commands, better translated as "I say to you" rather than "I advise you" (Acts 5:38).

One of Gamaliel's most notable moments occurs in Acts 5, where his intervention saved the apostles from being sentenced to death. Instead, they were flogged, a much lighter sentence (Acts 5:38-40). His ability to influence even the more severe Sadducees showcased his remarkable sway over the Sanhedrin.

Understanding Gamaliel's teachings sheds light on his profound impact on Paul of Tarsus, his most famous student. Like his teacher, Paul mentored young believers, reached out to Jews in the Diaspora, included Gentiles in his ministry, and used the Greek translation of the Scriptures. Gamaliel's influence on Paul is evident in Paul's inclusive approach to ministry and emphasis on education.

Modern Application:

Gamaliel's legacy of wisdom, leniency, and inclusion remains relevant today. In our lives, we can follow his example by showing compassion and seeking understanding in our relationships and interactions. Like Gamaliel, we are called to be mentors and guides, using the wisdom we have gained to influence others for the better. His emphasis on cultural inclusivity and openness to Gentiles challenges us to be more accepting of others, especially those different from ourselves. Just as Gamaliel shaped the course of history by mentoring Paul, we too can leave a lasting impact by investing in others and encouraging them in their walk of faith.

Reflection Questions:

- How can you practice leniency and compassion in your daily interactions, as Gamaliel did?
- In what ways can you mentor or influence others, using your experiences and knowledge?

- Are there areas of your life where you struggle with inclusivity or understanding others from different backgrounds? How can Gamaliel's example challenge you to grow in this area?

Prayer Focus:

- Pray for the wisdom to be a compassionate leader and mentor to others, just as Gamaliel was to Paul.
- Ask God to help you embrace inclusivity and understanding in your relationships, especially with those who are different from you.
- Pray for opportunities to influence others in positive ways, using the wisdom and experience God has given you.

Summary and Key Takeaways:

- **Key Takeaway 1:** Gamaliel's legacy of leniency, wisdom, and inclusivity shaped the Pharisaic movement and influenced early Christianity through Paul.
- **Key Takeaway 2:** Gamaliel's emphasis on compassion and tolerance challenges us to be more understanding and accepting of others.
- **Key Takeaway 3:** Like Gamaliel, we are called to mentor and guide others, using the wisdom we have gained to leave a lasting impact on those around us.

Gamaliel's life shows that influence is not always about power or control but about leading with wisdom, compassion, and openness. His impact on Paul and, ultimately, on the spread of the Gospel reminds us that God can use our lives to shape others in ways we may not even realize. By living out these principles in our own lives, we allow God to work through us to leave a lasting legacy of faith. Pray for a heart that is open to new insights and perspectives, just as Saul was shaped by his time with Gamaliel.

Summary and Key Takeaway:

- **Key Takeaway 1:** Saul's journey from Tarsus to Jerusalem was not only a physical voyage but a transformative period of growth and preparation that shaped his future as Paul, the apostle.
- **Key Takeaway 2:** The mentorship and rigorous study Saul experienced under Gamaliel provided him with the foundational knowledge that would later influence his ministry and theological writings.
- **Key Takeaway 3:** We, too, are called to embrace times of learning and growth, seeking wisdom and guidance from mentors and being open to transformation.

Saul's journey to Jerusalem represents a transformative time in his life, filled with scenic beauty, intellectual rigor, and spiritual anticipation. The knowledge and experiences he gained during his time studying under Gamaliel were instrumental in shaping him into Paul, the apostle who would leave a lasting legacy in both the Jewish and Christian faiths. Saul's story reminds us that every journey of transformation is marked by learning, growth, and preparation for what lies ahead.

Chapter Five

Paul's Conversion
A Continual Reminder of God's Transformative Power

The sun was at its peak, casting an intense light on the arid landscape surrounding the road to Damascus. A man named Saul, a fervent persecutor of Christians, journeyed with a singular purpose: to arrest those who followed Jesus. Little did he know that his life was about to be transformed by one divine moment.

Saul, a devout Pharisee, had built his life on strict adherence to the law and an unyielding belief that he was defending the true faith. His zeal drove him to great lengths to suppress what he saw as a dangerous sect. With letters of authority from the high priest, Saul was determined to root out this new movement, but the plan of the risen Christ would radically alter his mission.

As Saul and his companions traveled along the dusty road, a light from heaven suddenly enveloped them. It was brighter than the sun, blinding and overwhelming. Saul fell to the ground, his heart pounding in his chest. Then he heard a voice, clear and unmistakable: "Saul, Saul, why do you persecute me?"

"Who are you, Lord?" Saul asked, trembling.

"I am Jesus, whom you are persecuting," the voice replied. In that moment, Saul's life was upended. The realization that the Jesus he was persecuting was indeed alive and divine shattered his previous convictions.

When the light faded, Saul was left blind. His companions, speechless and awestruck, led him by the hand into Damascus. For three days, Saul neither ate nor drank, his sightless eyes reflecting his inner turmoil and the dawning awareness of his misguided fervor.

In Damascus, a disciple named Ananias received a vision from the Lord. "Go to the house of Judas on Straight Street and ask for a man from Tarsus named Saul, for he is praying." Understandably, Ananias was hesitant. He knew of Saul's reputation and the harm he had inflicted on the followers of Jesus.

But the Lord reassured him, "Go! This man is my chosen instrument to proclaim my name to the Gentiles and their kings and to the people of Israel. I will show him how much he must suffer for my name."

With faith and courage, Ananias obeyed. He found Saul, laid his hands on him, and said, "Brother Saul, the Lord—Jesus, who appeared to you on the road as you were coming here—has sent me so that you may see again and be filled with the Holy Spirit." Immediately, something like scales fell from Saul's eyes, and he could see again. He arose and was baptized, filled with the Holy Spirit, and nourished both in body and spirit.

This one divine moment on the road to Damascus changed everything for Saul. His fervor and zeal were redirected from persecuting Christians to proclaiming the gospel of Christ. Renamed Paul, he became one of the most influential apostles, spreading the message of Jesus far and wide. His letters, filled with theological depth and pastoral care, would later form a significant part of the New Testament.

Paul's conversion story is a powerful testament to the transformative power of encountering the risen Christ. It reminds us that no one is beyond the reach of God's grace. One moment in His presence can change the direction of a life, turning a persecutor into a preacher, a zealot into an apostle, and a sinner into a saint.

The story of Paul's conversion encourages us to remain open to divine interruptions in our own lives. Just as Paul's encounter with Christ redefined his mission and purpose, so can our encounters with God.

Each divine moment is an opportunity for transformation, renewal, and a deeper understanding of His will for our lives.

In the end, Paul's story is not just about a dramatic conversion; it's about the relentless pursuit of a loving God who sees potential where we see failure, and who calls each of us to a higher purpose. One divine moment truly can change everything!

MODERN APPLICATION:

Paul's dramatic encounter with Christ serves as a reminder that God can transform even the most unlikely people. In our busy, controlled lives, we often resist interruptions, but divine moments may come unexpectedly, bringing a new sense of purpose and calling. Whether through prayer, scripture, or life events, we should be open to these moments of transformation and allow God to redirect us, just as He did with Paul.

Reflection Questions:

- Have you experienced a "divine moment" in your life? How did it change you?
- Are you open to God interrupting your plans and guiding you toward a new direction or purpose?
- How can you respond with obedience and faith, like Ananias, when called to participate in someone else's transformation?

Prayer Focus:

- Pray for openness to God's transformative power in your life, even when it comes unexpectedly.
- Ask God to give you the courage and faith to respond to divine interruptions and follow His guidance.
- Thank God for the grace that reaches even the most unlikely

hearts and for the way He works in our lives, transforming us for His purpose.

Summary and Key Takeaways:

- **Key Takeaway 1:** Paul's conversion on the road to Damascus is a powerful example of how one divine moment can change a life forever, showing that no one is beyond the reach of God's grace.
- **Key Takeaway 2:** God often works through unexpected interruptions in our lives, transforming our mission and purpose just as He did for Paul.
- **Key Takeaway 3:** Sharing in others' transformations, like Ananias, reminds us that God uses us to bring about His work in the lives of others.

Paul's story teaches us that transformation can happen at any moment, in any life. Whether it's through a direct encounter with Christ or the guidance of others, each divine moment has the power to redirect our lives and align us with God's higher purpose. Let us remain open to these moments, trusting in the boundless grace that can change everything.

Chapter Six

Retelling The Story
How Important Is It?

The apostle Paul, once known as Saul of Tarsus, is a towering figure in Christian history, not only for his extensive missionary work and epistles but also for his dramatic conversion story. This narrative of transformation from a persecutor of Christians to a fervent apostle is repeatedly recounted by Paul throughout his letters and in the Book of Acts. Paul's continual reminder of his conversion serves as a powerful testament to God's grace and a crucial lesson for all believers: never forget where you have come from and where Christ has brought you to.

Paul's conversion on the road to Damascus is a cornerstone of his identity and ministry. In Acts 9, we read about how a bright light from heaven blinded him, and a voice—Jesus—asked, "Saul, Saul, why do you persecute me?" This profound encounter led to Paul's spiritual rebirth and set him on a path of relentless evangelism. He frequently referenced, as in Acts 22 and 26, this transformative experience in his testimonies, underscoring its importance in his life and mission.

One might wonder why Paul was so insistent on retelling his conversion story. The answer lies in the power of testimony. By reminding others of his past and how Christ radically changed his life, Paul demonstrated the boundless reach of God's grace. His story was not just a personal narrative but a tool to inspire faith and hope in others. It was a living example of how God can transform anyone, regardless of their past.

GOD'S QUILL CRAFTING YOUR STORY IN DIVINE HARMONY

For contemporary believers, Paul's example holds a vital lesson. It is essential to reflect on our own spiritual journeys and acknowledge the work Christ has done in our lives. By remembering where we have come from and the transformation we have undergone, we can maintain a posture of humility and gratitude. This reflection helps us stay grounded in our faith, continually aware of God's mercy and love.

Sharing our stories with others, as Paul did, can be a powerful witness. Our testimonies, like Paul's, can encourage and strengthen others in their faith journeys. They remind us and those around us that God is always at work, transforming lives and drawing people closer to Him.

Paul's continual reminder of his conversion is not just a historical recount; it is a model for all believers. By keeping our own spiritual transformations in view and sharing them with others, we celebrate God's ongoing work in our lives and inspire others to trust in His transformative power. Let us remember, reflect, and rejoice in the incredible journey of faith that Christ has brought us through.

The apostle Paul, formerly Saul of Tarsus, is one of the most influential figures in Christian history, known not only for his missionary work and epistles but also for his remarkable conversion. His transformation from a fierce persecutor of Christians to a dedicated apostle is a narrative Paul frequently revisits in his letters and in the Book of Acts. Paul's repeated references to his conversion serve as a profound testament to God's grace and a crucial lesson for all believers: never forget where you have come from and where Christ has brought you.

Modern Application:
Paul's story reminds us that no one is beyond the reach of God's grace, and transformation is possible for everyone. It is important for us to reflect on how Christ has worked in our lives and to share those stories with others. When we remember and tell our own conversion stories, it keeps us humble and points others toward God's power to change lives, no matter how unlikely the change may seem.

Reflection Questions:

- How has your life changed since encountering Christ?
- Do you share your personal testimony with others to encourage them in their own faith?
- What can you do to remain mindful of God's ongoing work of transformation in your life?

Prayer Focus:

- Ask God to give you opportunities to reflect on your spiritual journey and recognize His transformative work in your life.
- Pray for the courage and wisdom to share your testimony with others, that they may be encouraged and strengthened in their own faith.
- Thank God for His grace that reaches beyond our past, continually shaping us into who He calls us to be.

Summary and Key Takeaway:

- **Key Takeaway 1:** Paul's conversion from persecutor to apostle is a powerful reminder of God's ability to transform anyone's life, regardless of their past.
- **Key Takeaway 2:** Paul's continual reflection on his transformation illustrates the importance of remembering where we've come from and how Christ has worked in us.
- **Key Takeaway 3:** Sharing our stories of transformation can encourage others in their faith, reminding them that God is actively working to transform lives.

Paul's conversion story is not merely a historical recount but a model for all believers. His reminder to never forget his transformation encourages us to reflect on our own journeys, fostering humility and

GOD'S QUILL CRAFTING YOUR STORY IN DIVINE HARMONY

gratitude. By sharing these stories, we testify to God's grace and inspire others to trust in His transformative power. Let us, like Paul, remember, reflect, and share the incredible work of Christ in our lives.

Chapter Seven

Contrast Of Faiths
When Integrity Matters

In Acts 4:32-36, we are given a vivid snapshot of the early Christian community that highlights an extraordinary spirit of unity and generosity. The believers were described as being "of one heart and soul," sharing everything they had so that "there was not a needy person among them." This wasn't just an act of charity—it was a way of life that demonstrated their deep commitment to one another. The early Christians were willing to sell their possessions and lands to ensure that every member of the community's needs were met. This selfless, communal lifestyle was a powerful expression of their faith and a reflection of the transformative power of the Holy Spirit in their lives.

One of the most notable examples of this spirit of generosity was Barnabas. Originally named Joseph, he was a Levite from Cyprus who sold a field he owned and brought the proceeds to the apostles. His act of selflessness was so striking that it earned him the name Barnabas, which means "son of encouragement." Barnabas's actions embodied the very essence of the early church's values—sacrifice, generosity, and a deep commitment to the community. He didn't seek personal recognition or praise but acted out of genuine love for others, setting a high standard for what it meant to live as a disciple of Jesus. His life was a testament to the power of living in alignment with God's will, demonstrating that true discipleship is not just about words but actions that reflect a heart fully devoted to God and His people.

GOD'S QUILL CRAFTING YOUR STORY IN DIVINE HARMONY

However, the narrative takes a dramatic turn in Acts 5 with the story of Ananias and Sapphira. This couple also sold a piece of property, but instead of following Barnabas's example, they secretly kept back part of the proceeds while claiming to have donated the entire amount to the apostles. Their deception wasn't just a lie to the community but, as Peter declared, a lie to the Holy Spirit. This stark contrast between Barnabas's authentic generosity and the couple's deceitful actions serves as a powerful reminder of the importance of integrity and transparency in the Christian life. The Holy Spirit's presence in the early church was transformative, but it also demanded sincerity and truthfulness.

Ananias and Sapphira's desire for recognition without the accompanying sacrifice resulted in a tragic end—both were struck down for their deceit. Their story sent a sobering message to the early church about the seriousness of lying to God and attempting to deceive the community. Their actions were motivated by pride and a desire to appear more generous than they actually were, while Barnabas's heart was truly aligned with God's purpose.

The contrast between Barnabas and Ananias and Sapphira challenges us to examine the motivations behind our actions. Barnabas's generosity flowed from his deep faith and his commitment to the well-being of others, while Ananias and Sapphira were driven by a desire for outward recognition without the inward sacrifice. This passage invites us to reflect on our own hearts, encouraging us to follow Barnabas's example of genuine generosity and a sincere desire to build up the community of believers.

Ultimately, these stories serve as powerful reminders of the values that should guide our lives as followers of Christ: authenticity, generosity, integrity, and a heart that seeks to honor God above all. Barnabas's life demonstrated the transformative power of the Holy Spirit, and the tragic story of Ananias and Sapphira warns us of the dangers of hypocrisy and pride in our walk with God.

Reflection Questions:

1. In what ways can I practice the kind of generosity and selflessness that Barnabas exemplified?
2. Are there areas in my life where I am seeking recognition without truly sacrificing for others?
3. How can I be more transparent and authentic in my relationships with God and my community?
4. What motivates my actions—genuine love for others or a desire for approval?

Modern Application:

In today's world, where individualism often takes precedence over community, the early church's example of unity and generosity challenges us to rethink our priorities. Barnabas's actions remind us that true discipleship involves sacrificial living. Whether it's our time, resources, or energy, God calls us to give freely for the sake of others. In contrast, the story of Ananias and Sapphira warns against giving for the sake of appearances. Integrity, both in our relationships with others and in our walk with God, is essential. We are called to live with open hearts, offering not just material help but also encouragement and spiritual support to those in need.

Prayer Focus:

- Ask God to give you a heart like Barnabas—one that is selflessly generous, encouraging, and committed to the well-being of others.
- Pray for the wisdom to examine your motivations and the courage to live a life marked by authenticity and integrity.
- Seek the Holy Spirit's guidance in identifying opportunities to serve and uplift your community, and ask for strength to resist the temptation to seek recognition or approval from others.

Summary:

GOD'S QUILL CRAFTING YOUR STORY IN DIVINE HARMONY

Acts 4:32-36 paints a beautiful picture of the early Christian community, united in heart and soul, sharing all they had to ensure that no one was in need. Barnabas, through his selfless generosity, became a shining example of what it means to live a life of discipleship. In contrast, the story of Ananias and Sapphira in Acts 5 serves as a warning about the dangers of deceit and hypocrisy. These passages challenge us to reflect on our own motivations and encourage us to live lives marked by authenticity, integrity, and generosity.

Key Takeaways:

- **Unity and Generosity:** The early Christian community was united in both heart and purpose, willing to give up their own possessions to meet the needs of others.
- **Barnabas's Example:** Barnabas embodied the values of the early church through his sacrificial giving, earning the name "son of encouragement."
- **Integrity Matters:** The story of Ananias and Sapphira serves as a reminder that deceit, especially in spiritual matters, has serious consequences.
- **Examine Your Heart:** We are called to reflect on our motivations and ensure that our actions are driven by genuine love for God and others, not a desire for recognition.
- **Discipleship in Action:** True discipleship requires more than words—it demands actions that reflect a heart fully committed to God and His people.

Chapter Eight

Divine Commission
When God Calls

The journey began in the bustling city of Antioch, a thriving center of early Christian activity and mission. It was here that Barnabas and Saul, along with a group of prophets and teachers, gathered for a prayer meeting. However, this was no ordinary gathering; it was a time of worship, fasting, and profound communion with God. As these leaders devoted themselves to prayer, the Holy Spirit spoke clearly and directly: "Set apart for Me Barnabas and Saul for the work to which I have called them" (Acts 13:2). This was not merely a call to action but a divine commissioning, a sending forth under the authority and empowerment of the Holy Spirit. After further fasting and prayer, the church laid hands on Barnabas and Saul, commissioning them to embark on a mission that would change the world.

Accompanied by John Mark, Barnabas and Saul set sail for Cyprus. This journey held special meaning for Barnabas, as he was returning to his homeland, but this time with a new mission—to proclaim the Gospel of Jesus Christ. Upon arriving in Salamis, they immediately began preaching in the Jewish synagogues. As they moved through the island, they eventually reached Paphos, where a significant confrontation took place. They encountered a sorcerer named Elymas, who actively opposed their efforts to share the Gospel with Sergius Paulus, the Roman proconsul. Filled with the Holy Spirit, Saul (who from this point is referred to as Paul) rebuked Elymas, causing him to go blind. This miraculous display of God's power led to the conversion of Sergius

Paulus, demonstrating the supremacy of the Gospel over darkness and opposition.

From Cyprus, Barnabas and Paul traveled to Perga in Pamphylia. It was here that John Mark left them, a decision that would later cause a division between Barnabas and Paul. Despite this setback, the two missionaries pressed on to Antioch in Pisidia. Here, Paul delivered a powerful sermon in the synagogue, recounting the history of Israel and proclaiming Jesus as the long-awaited Messiah. His message stirred the hearts of both Jews and Gentiles, and many came to faith. However, not everyone was receptive. Opposition arose from some Jewish leaders, and the apostles were driven out of the region. Undeterred, they shook the dust from their feet—a symbolic act of protest—and continued to Iconium.

In Iconium, their preaching was again met with both great success and fierce resistance. A significant number of Jews and Gentiles believed in their message, but a plot to stone them forced Barnabas and Paul to flee to Lystra and Derbe in Lycaonia. In Lystra, a miraculous event unfolded when Paul healed a man who had been lame from birth. The people, astonished by the miracle, believed that Barnabas and Paul were gods—Barnabas being Zeus and Paul being Hermes—and they attempted to offer sacrifices to them. Deeply distressed, Barnabas and Paul tore their clothes and rushed to stop the people, insisting that they were mere men bringing the good news of the living God.

Their journey continued to Derbe, where they preached the Gospel and made many disciples. Retracing their steps, they returned to Lystra, Iconium, and Antioch in Pisidia. At each stop, they not only preached but also strengthened the disciples, encouraging them to remain steadfast in their faith and appointing elders to lead the newly established churches. Their mission was more than just spreading the Gospel—it was about ensuring that these new believers had the foundation and leadership necessary to grow in their faith and build strong Christian communities.

Finally, Barnabas and Paul returned to Antioch, their starting point, where they reported to the church all that God had done through them, including how He had opened the door of faith to the Gentiles. This first missionary journey marked a significant expansion of the early church's mission, spreading the Gospel beyond the Jewish world and into the Gentile regions, fulfilling Jesus' command to take the message to the ends of the earth. The journey was characterized by divine guidance, miraculous signs, and unwavering dedication despite opposition and trials. Barnabas and Paul's steadfast faith and commitment laid a foundation for future missionary work and showed the unstoppable nature of the Gospel when empowered by the Holy Spirit.

Reflection Questions:

1. How does the example of Barnabas and Paul's obedience to the Holy Spirit challenge me in my own life?
2. In what ways do I experience opposition or challenges when I step out in faith? How can I remain steadfast like Barnabas and Paul?
3. How can I actively encourage and strengthen others in their faith, just as Barnabas and Paul did with the early Christian communities?
4. What areas of my life are in need of deeper surrender to the guidance of the Holy Spirit?

Modern Application:

In a fast-paced and self-centered world, the story of Barnabas and Paul challenges us to prioritize prayer, fasting, and seeking God's guidance in everything we do. Their journey teaches us the importance of obedience to the Holy Spirit, even when it leads us into uncharted territory or brings opposition. Just as they were sent to proclaim the Gospel and establish new communities of faith, we too are called to live as witnesses of Christ in our workplaces, homes, and neighborhoods. The courage of Barnabas and Paul in the face of rejection reminds us that the Gospel is powerful, and its message continues to change lives today. Our task, like theirs, is to remain faithful, trusting that God will lead, empower, and protect us as we share His love with others.

Prayer Focus:

- Pray for the courage to follow the Holy Spirit's leading in your life, even when it's difficult or requires stepping out of your comfort zone.
- Ask for the faithfulness of Barnabas and Paul as you seek to share the Gospel in your daily life.
- Pray for strength to endure opposition and for the wisdom to build up others in their faith, encouraging them just as Barnabas and Paul did with the early Christians.
- Ask God to open doors of opportunity for you to spread His love and message to others.

Summary:

The first missionary journey of Barnabas and Paul was a groundbreaking mission that expanded the reach of the Gospel beyond the Jewish community to include Gentiles. The journey began in Antioch with the Holy Spirit's direct instruction and continued through Cyprus, Perga, Antioch in Pisidia, Iconium, Lystra, and Derbe. Despite opposition, persecution, and setbacks, Barnabas and Paul faithfully proclaimed the Gospel, performed miracles, and established strong Christian communities. Their journey not only demonstrated the unstoppable power of the Gospel but also laid the foundation for future missionary work. Their steadfastness, obedience, and reliance on the Holy Spirit serve as powerful examples for believers today.

Key Takeaways:

- **Divine Commissioning:** The mission of Barnabas and Paul was not just an idea but a clear call from the Holy Spirit, reminding us to seek God's direction in all things.

- **Power of the Gospel:** Their journey demonstrated the power of the Gospel to change lives, as seen in the conversion of both Jews and Gentiles and the miracles they performed.
- **Opposition and Perseverance:** The mission was not without challenges, but Barnabas and Paul persevered, trusting in God's guidance and strength.
- **Strengthening the Church:** Their work wasn't just about evangelism—it was about building up and encouraging the early Christian communities and ensuring they had strong leadership.
- **Faithfulness:** The faithfulness of Barnabas and Paul to their mission, despite setbacks, is a powerful reminder that God's work is unstoppable when empowered by the Holy Spirit.

Chapter Nine

When Disagreement Occurs
Can Any Good Come From it?

In Acts 15, we witness a pivotal moment in the early church—a sharp disagreement between two of its most prominent leaders, Paul and Barnabas. This conflict, while difficult and emotional, ultimately played a significant role in the expansion of the gospel and the growth of the early Christian movement. The disagreement centered around John Mark, a young man who had accompanied Paul and Barnabas on their first missionary journey. However, John Mark had left them in Pamphylia (Acts 13:13) and returned home, which Paul saw as an act of desertion.

When Paul and Barnabas were planning their next missionary journey to visit the churches they had planted, Barnabas suggested that they take John Mark with them again. Paul strongly disagreed, feeling that John Mark's previous actions made him unreliable for the demands of the mission ahead (Acts 15:37-38). The Greek word "paroxysm," used to describe their contention, indicates that this was not just a mild disagreement but a sharp and emotional dispute. As a result, Paul and Barnabas parted ways. Barnabas took John Mark and sailed to Cyprus, while Paul chose Silas and continued his missionary work in Syria and Cilicia (Acts 15:39-41).

Although this division may appear regrettable, God used it to multiply the spread of the gospel. Instead of one missionary team, there were now two, and the message of Christ reached even more regions.

Barnabas, true to his character as an encourager and mentor, saw potential in John Mark despite his earlier failure. He understood that spiritual growth often requires patience, guidance, and second chances. By taking John Mark under his wing, Barnabas played a key role in his spiritual development. This investment bore great fruit, as John Mark later became a trusted leader in the early church. In fact, years later, Paul himself acknowledged John Mark's value when he wrote, "Get Mark and bring him with you, because he is helpful to me in my ministry" (2 Timothy 4:11). This demonstrates that Barnabas's faith in John Mark had been well placed, and over time, John Mark matured into a reliable and effective partner in ministry.

Meanwhile, Paul needed someone who was ready to endure the intense challenges of missionary work, and Silas was the perfect choice. Silas had already proven himself a courageous and faithful leader (Acts 15:22). Together, Paul and Silas embarked on a journey filled with hardship—imprisonment, beatings, and persecution—but through it all, they remained steadfast, and the gospel continued to spread (Acts 16).

While the conflict between Paul and Barnabas was unfortunate, it was not without purpose. Their separation led to the gospel being preached in more regions than if they had stayed together. Barnabas's mentoring of John Mark helped shape him into a valuable leader, while Paul and Silas brought the message of Christ to new places, enduring persecution with faith and resilience.

This story serves as a powerful reminder that even our conflicts and disagreements can be used by God for a greater purpose. When handled with grace and faith, moments of division can lead to growth, maturity, and the furthering of God's kingdom in ways that we may not immediately recognize.

While we don't know much about what happened to Barnabas after this event, we see his lasting influence through John Mark, who went on to write the Gospel of Mark. Only when we see God's full plan revealed in eternity will we fully understand how these moments shaped the future of the church.

Reflection Questions:

1. Have I ever experienced a disagreement that, though painful at the time, ultimately led to positive outcomes or growth in my spiritual life?
2. In what ways can I show grace and patience to those who may have stumbled or failed, as Barnabas did with John Mark?
3. How do I handle conflict in my relationships? Do I seek God's greater purpose, even in difficult situations?
4. How can I remain steadfast and faithful, like Paul and Silas, in the face of hardships and challenges?

Modern Application:

This story speaks to us today about the importance of both mentoring and resilience in ministry. Like Barnabas, we are called to encourage and support others, even when they have stumbled or failed in the past. Spiritual growth is a journey, and we all need grace and second chances along the way. Barnabas's faith in John Mark transformed him into a future leader, reminding us of the impact we can have when we invest in others.

On the other hand, Paul and Silas's partnership demonstrates the importance of perseverance in the face of hardship. The Christian life is not without challenges, but when we remain faithful and committed, God uses our efforts for His glory. The division between Paul and Barnabas, though painful, reminds us that God can work through even our conflicts to accomplish His purposes, and what seems like a setback can often lead to greater growth and multiplication in ministry.

Prayer Focus:

- Pray for wisdom and grace in handling conflicts in your life.
- Ask God to help you see His greater purpose in difficult

situations and to trust that He can use even disagreements for His glory.
- Pray for the patience and encouragement to support those who are struggling in their faith, and for the resilience to continue serving faithfully, no matter the hardships you face.
- Ask for the humility to learn from others and the strength to build up those around you, just as Barnabas did with John Mark.

Summary:

In Acts 15, we see a significant disagreement between Paul and Barnabas over John Mark's role in their missionary work. While Paul did not want to bring John Mark along due to his previous desertion, Barnabas saw potential in him and chose to mentor him. This conflict led to their separation, with Barnabas taking John Mark to Cyprus and Paul partnering with Silas for further missionary work. Despite the division, God used it to expand the reach of the gospel. Barnabas's investment in John Mark eventually bore fruit, as John Mark became a trusted leader, while Paul and Silas continued to spread the gospel despite persecution. This story reminds us that God can use our conflicts to accomplish His greater purposes, and that grace, patience, and perseverance are vital in our Christian Walk.

Key Takeaways:

- **Mentorship and Encouragement:** Barnabas's willingness to give John Mark a second chance highlights the importance of investing in others and offering grace.
- **Perseverance in Hardship:** Paul and Silas exemplified steadfast faithfulness in the face of opposition, showing that God can work through trials to spread the gospel.
- **God's Greater Purpose:** Even conflicts and disagreements can be used by God to further His kingdom, multiplying efforts and

leading to growth in unexpected ways.
- **Growth Through Grace:** John Mark's transformation from someone Paul deemed unreliable to a valued partner in ministry demonstrates the power of encouragement and spiritual growth.
- **The Impact of Division:** Though painful, the separation of Paul and Barnabas ultimately led to the gospel reaching more regions, reminding us that God can use all situations for His glory.

Chapter Ten

The First Missionary Journey
Breaking New Ground

Paul's first missionary journey, as recounted in Acts 13-14, was a groundbreaking endeavor that significantly expanded the reach of the Gospel. This journey marked a key moment in Christian history, where the message of Christ was taken beyond the borders of Judea and into the Gentile world. The journey was full of challenges—opposition from religious leaders, rejection from some communities, and even physical danger. Yet Paul and his companions pressed on, driven by their deep conviction that they were called by God to spread the Gospel. They were empowered by the Holy Spirit and trusted that their labor would contribute to the growth of God's Kingdom.

Prayer and Sending in Acts 13: The Significance of Antioch

The journey began with prayer. In Acts 13, we see the church in Antioch gathered together for worship and fasting. It was in this atmosphere of prayer that the Holy Spirit spoke, instructing the church to "Set apart for Me Barnabas and Saul for the work to which I have called them" (Acts 13:2). This moment was crucial for Paul's ministry because it demonstrated that mission work must begin with prayer and reliance on the guidance of the Holy Spirit. Antioch was a thriving church, and the leaders recognized the importance of seeking God's direction before embarking on the challenging task of spreading the Gospel to unreached areas. This act of sending through prayer and fasting highlights the importance of being spiritually prepared for the mission ahead.

Challenges and Conflicts: The Difficulties Faced During the First Missionary Journey

Paul's journey was far from smooth. He faced opposition from Jewish leaders, rejection from Gentile communities, and even physical persecution, including being stoned and left for dead in Lystra (Acts 14:19). However, Paul's perseverance in the face of adversity was a testament to his faith. He believed that the hardships he encountered were part of fulfilling God's calling and would ultimately serve to advance the Kingdom of God. Every city Paul visited brought a mixture of success and conflict—some people embraced the Gospel, while others resisted it fiercely. These challenges were not signs of failure but indicators that the work of God was taking place.

Paul's example teaches us that opposition and difficulties should not deter us from stepping out in faith. Whether it's launching a new ministry, advocating for justice, or sharing our faith with others, breaking new ground often comes with spiritual and physical challenges. Like Paul, we must trust that God is with us in the journey, using every situation for His glory.

Modern Application

Paul's first missionary journey offers valuable lessons for modern believers. While we may not face physical persecution as Paul did, stepping out in faith to break new ground in our lives or communities still requires courage and perseverance. Today, breaking new ground could mean starting a new ministry in your church, advocating for justice in a difficult situation, or simply having a conversation with someone about your faith.

We live in a world where comfort and convenience are often prioritized, and stepping out in faith can feel uncomfortable or even risky. However, Paul's journey reminds us that God's call is often accompanied by challenges, and those challenges can be opportunities for growth and transformation. God uses these difficulties to shape our character, deepen our faith, and expand His Kingdom.

Whether you're starting a new project, moving into a new phase of life, or taking a stand for your beliefs, Paul's perseverance and reliance on the Holy Spirit serve as a powerful model. Like Paul, we are called to push beyond our comfort zones, trusting that God will guide us and provide the strength we need to face obstacles along the way.

Reflection Questions:

1. What new ground is God calling you to break in your life, ministry, or community?
2. How can you prepare spiritually and mentally to face the challenges that come with stepping out in faith?
3. Are there areas in your life where fear or discomfort is holding you back from answering God's call? How can you overcome those barriers?
4. How does Paul's reliance on prayer and the Holy Spirit challenge you in your personal life and ministry?

Actionable Steps:

1. This week, identify one area in your life where you feel God is calling you to step out in faith. It could be starting a conversation about your faith, volunteering for a cause you're passionate about, or initiating a new project in your workplace or community.
2. Take one bold step toward that challenge, trusting that God will guide you through the process. Remember that it's not about immediate success but about faithfully following God's direction.
3. Consider forming a prayer group or finding a mentor who can support you as you step into new areas of faith. Surrounding yourself with a community of believers will provide encouragement and accountability.

GOD'S QUILL CRAFTING YOUR STORY IN DIVINE HARMONY

Prayer Focus:

- Pray for boldness and perseverance as you step out in faith, asking God to give you the strength to face the challenges that come with breaking new ground.
- Ask for the Holy Spirit's guidance in discerning where God is leading you and the courage to take the necessary steps, even if they are difficult or uncomfortable.
- Pray for those who are facing persecution or hardships for their faith around the world, asking God to protect and empower them as they spread the Gospel.

Summary:

Paul's first missionary journey was a groundbreaking step in the spread of the Gospel, but it was also filled with opposition, rejection, and physical danger. Yet Paul and his companions, driven by their faith in God's mission, persevered and saw the Gospel take root in new regions. Their journey highlights the importance of prayer, reliance on the Holy Spirit, and the courage to face challenges. In our own lives, we are called to step out in faith, trusting that God will use the obstacles we face to grow His Kingdom and shape our spiritual walk.

Key Takeaways:

1. **Breaking new ground requires courage and perseverance** – Whether in ministry or personal life, stepping out in faith often comes with challenges, but these are opportunities for growth.
2. **Prayer is essential in mission work** – Paul's journey began with prayer and fasting, reminding us that every endeavor for God should be grounded in spiritual preparation.
3. **Challenges are part of God's plan** – Opposition and difficulties are not signs of failure but indicators that we are walking in God's will, and He will provide the strength to overcome.

4. **The Gospel is unstoppable when we rely on God** – Despite the challenges Paul faced, the message of Christ spread and transformed lives, showing the power of perseverance and faithfulness in God's mission.

Chapter Eleven

The Final Chapters
A Life Poured Out

As Paul neared the end of his life, he took the time to reflect on his journey and ministry, writing some of the most profound and personal letters in the New Testament. These final letters—like 2 Timothy—reveal a man at peace with the life he had lived, fully aware that he had given everything for the sake of Christ. Paul described his life as a "race well run" and a "good fight fought" (2 Timothy 4:7-8), offering a model of how to live with intention, perseverance, and purpose. His reflections encourage believers to examine their own lives and consider what kind of legacy they will leave behind.

Paul's legacy was not one of wealth, power, or worldly success. Instead, it was a legacy of faithfulness, sacrifice, and devotion to spreading the Gospel. He poured himself out for the cause of Christ, investing in people and building the early church. His letters continue to inspire and challenge believers, reminding us that our lives are part of something much greater than ourselves. Paul's reflections are an invitation to live with the end in mind—to pour ourselves out in service to God and others, leaving behind a legacy that honors Him.

Paul's Final Days: The Significance of His Last Letters

Paul's final letters, particularly 2 Timothy, give us a glimpse into his heart as he prepared for the end of his earthly journey. Written from a Roman prison, Paul knew that his time was short. Yet, his words are filled with peace and confidence. He wasn't focused on the suffering he endured or the approaching end of his life; instead, he was focused on the faithfulness of God and the legacy he was leaving behind.

In 2 Timothy 4:6, Paul writes, "For I am already being poured out as a drink offering, and the time of my departure is at hand." This imagery of being poured out reflects Paul's life of complete surrender and sacrifice for the Gospel. He had given everything he had—his time, his energy, his love, and ultimately his life—for the sake of Christ. Paul's example challenges us to consider how we are pouring ourselves out for the Kingdom of God.

Paul also expresses confidence in the reward that awaits him, saying, "There is laid up for me the crown of righteousness, which the Lord, the righteous judge, will give to me on that day" (2 Timothy 4:8). This eternal perspective shaped Paul's entire life. He knew that his true reward wasn't found in earthly success or recognition but in the approval of his Savior. Paul's life was a testimony to living with an eternal perspective, and his final letters encourage us to do the same.

The Legacy of Paul: Inspiration for Believers Today

Paul's life continues to inspire and challenge believers today. His legacy wasn't about building an empire or achieving personal greatness; it was about making an eternal impact through faithfulness to God's call. Paul invested in people—mentoring leaders like Timothy, establishing churches, and writing letters that continue to guide and shape the Christian faith.

In our modern context, Paul's reflections challenge us to consider what we are pouring our lives into. Are we investing in things that will last? Are we focusing on what truly matters—our faith, our relationships, and our impact on others? The world often encourages us to prioritize temporary achievements, wealth, and success. However, Paul's life reminds us that our true legacy is found in the ways we live out our faith and serve others.

Today, pouring ourselves out might mean mentoring someone in their spiritual journey, serving our community, or simply being present for our family and friends. It's about living with purpose and making decisions that reflect our faith and values. Paul's life challenges us to live intentionally, recognizing that how we live now will echo into eternity. He encourages us to focus on leaving a legacy of faith, love, and service that will have a lasting impact on those around us.

Modern Application: Living with the End in Mind

Paul's reflections on his life encourage us to live with intentionality and focus on what truly matters. Whether we are just beginning our journey or nearing the end, we are invited to consider our own legacy. In a world that often prioritizes the temporary—wealth, status, and personal success—Paul's life reminds us that the true measure of a life well-lived is found in faithfulness to God and service to others.

Living with the end in mind doesn't mean obsessing over death or dwelling on what we haven't accomplished. Instead, it's about recognizing that each day is an opportunity to pour ourselves out in ways that matter for eternity. Whether through small acts of kindness, investing in relationships, or serving others, we can build a legacy that reflects our faith and honors God.

For many, this might involve taking time to mentor someone, investing in the spiritual growth of a younger believer, or serving in a ministry that impacts lives for Christ. It might mean re-evaluating priorities to ensure that our time, talents, and resources are being used for God's purposes rather than our own. Like Paul, we are called to live with the awareness that our lives are part of God's greater story, and we have the opportunity to contribute to that story in meaningful ways.

Reflection Questions:

1. What kind of legacy are you building today? How do you want to be remembered by those who know you?
2. In what ways are you pouring yourself out for the Kingdom of God? How are you investing in the lives of others?
3. Are there areas of your life where you need to re-evaluate your

priorities to focus more on eternal matters rather than temporary pursuits?
4. How does Paul's example of living with an eternal perspective challenge you in your current season of life?

Actionable Steps:

1. **Reflect on Your Legacy**: Take time this week to reflect on what kind of legacy you are building. Write down the values and priorities that are most important to you and how you can align your life with those values.
2. **Make a Change**: Identify one area in your life where you can make a change to invest more in your faith, relationships, or acts of service. This might mean mentoring someone, serving in a new way, or simply being more intentional with your time.
3. **Share Your Story**: Consider writing a letter to someone you care about, sharing how God has worked in your life and encouraging them in their faith journey.
4. **Focus on Eternity**: Each day, make a conscious effort to live with an eternal perspective. Ask yourself how your actions, decisions, and priorities align with God's purposes for your life.

Prayer Focus:

- **Pray for Wisdom**: Ask God for the wisdom to focus on what truly matters and to live each day with purpose and intentionality. Pray for discernment in making decisions that honor Him.
- **Pray for Strength**: Ask God for the strength to pour yourself out in service to Him and others. Pray for the courage to embrace the opportunities He gives you to make an impact.
- **Pray for Legacy**: Pray that your life would be a reflection of

God's love and grace and that you would leave behind a legacy of faith that influences others for Christ.

Summary:

Paul's final reflections on his life and ministry challenge us to live with the end in mind. His legacy was not one of personal achievement but of faithfulness, sacrifice, and service to God and others. As we consider our own lives, Paul's example encourages us to invest in what truly matters—our relationships, our faith, and our impact on others. By living with an eternal perspective, we can leave behind a legacy that honors God and influences those around us for Christ.

Key Takeaways:

1. **A Life Poured Out**: Paul's life was one of complete surrender and sacrifice for the sake of the Gospel. His example challenges us to pour ourselves out for God's Kingdom.
2. **Legacy of Faith**: Our legacy is not defined by worldly success but by the ways we invest in others, live out our faith, and serve God with our time, talents, and resources.
3. **Eternal Perspective**: Living with the end in mind means focusing on what truly matters—our relationship with God and how we impact others for eternity.
4. **Intentional Living**: Each day is an opportunity to live intentionally, making choices that reflect our values and build a legacy of faith and love.

Chapter Twelve

The Continuing Narrative
Paul's Story and Ours

The story of Paul, one of the most significant figures in early Christianity, didn't end with his death, and neither does ours. Paul's life was part of a much larger narrative—God's unfolding plan for humanity. Even after Paul's martyrdom, the impact of his ministry continued through the churches he planted, the letters he wrote, and the disciples he mentored. In the same way, God is continually writing new chapters in our lives, and we are invited to be active participants in this ongoing divine narrative.

Just as God worked through Paul, He is also working in and through us today. Our lives are part of a greater story, a story that is still being written. Each day presents new opportunities to contribute to this unfolding narrative—through acts of love, service, faithfulness, and trust in God's authorship. The chapters of our lives reflect God's grace, guidance, and purpose, as we align ourselves with His will and participate in His mission in the world.

Paul's Story: A Model of Faithfulness

Paul's life was marked by radical transformation. Once a persecutor of Christians, he became one of the most dedicated and influential apostles, spreading the Gospel across the Roman Empire. Paul's story is not just about his dramatic conversion on the road to Damascus (Acts 9), but about his continual faithfulness to God's call, even in the face of suffering, imprisonment, and ultimately, death.

GOD'S QUILL CRAFTING YOUR STORY IN DIVINE HARMONY

Throughout his ministry, Paul's life was characterized by a profound sense of purpose. He knew that God was the author of his story, and he trusted in the divine plan, even when circumstances were difficult. Whether he was preaching in synagogues, establishing churches, writing letters from prison, or defending the faith before kings, Paul recognized that each moment of his life was part of God's greater plan.

In 2 Timothy 4:6-8, Paul reflects on his life and ministry, saying, "I have fought the good fight, I have finished the race, I have kept the faith." These words reveal Paul's understanding that his life was part of something much larger than himself. He had faithfully completed the work God had given him, and he was confident that his story would continue through the lives of those he had influenced and the churches he had planted.

The Continuing Narrative: God Writing Our Story

Like Paul, we are each part of God's ongoing story. While we may not have the same calling or experiences as Paul, we share the same invitation to participate in God's divine narrative. Each day, God gives us the opportunity to write new chapters in our lives, and we are co-authors with Him in this journey.

God's story in our lives isn't limited to grand moments of conversion or public ministry. It is also written in the everyday acts of love, kindness, and faithfulness. Whether we are raising a family, serving in our community, working in our jobs, or sharing our faith with a neighbor, each action is a contribution to the story that God is writing in and through us.

The chapters of our lives include moments of joy, triumph, and success, but they also include challenges, trials, and setbacks. Paul's life reminds us that these difficult chapters are not wasted; they are integral to the story. It is often in these moments that God's grace shines most brightly, shaping us into the people He has called us to be and preparing us for the next chapter He is writing.

Modern Application: Living in God's Story Today

Today, we are living in the unfolding story of God's plan. Just as Paul's story didn't end with his death, our story doesn't end with one chapter or even with our earthly life. We are invited to live with the awareness that each day is an opportunity to contribute to God's greater narrative. Whether through acts of love, service, faithfulness, or simply trusting in God's guidance, we are called to actively participate in the story God is writing in our lives.

For example, starting a new ministry, sharing the Gospel with a friend, or serving those in need are all ways we can participate in God's ongoing narrative. Even small, everyday actions—like showing kindness to a coworker, offering a listening ear to someone who is hurting, or spending time in prayer—are significant contributions to the story of God's work in the world.

The modern world often emphasizes individual achievement, success, and control over one's destiny. However, as Christians, we are called to recognize that our lives are part of something much greater than ourselves. We are part of God's story, and our role is not to be the sole author of our lives but to trust in God's authorship and follow His leading.

Reflection Questions:

1. How do you see God writing your story today? What new chapters might He be inviting you to participate in?
2. In what areas of your life do you need to trust more fully in God's authorship rather than trying to write your own story?
3. How can you actively contribute to God's narrative through your actions, relationships, and choices?
4. What chapters in your life have been difficult, and how might God be using those challenges to shape your future story?

Actionable Steps:

1. **Reflect on Your Story**: Take time this week to reflect on the

story God is writing in your life. Write down the chapters that have already been written—both the joyful and the challenging ones. Consider how God has been at work in each of these moments, shaping your faith and your character.
2. **Pray About the Future**: Ask God to reveal the chapters yet to come. Pray for the courage to embrace whatever new opportunities, challenges, or changes He may be leading you toward.
3. **Share Your Story**: Consider sharing your story with someone else. Whether it's a close friend, a family member, or someone in your church community, sharing how God has been at work in your life can encourage others in their own faith journeys.
4. **Participate in God's Story**: This week, look for one specific way you can actively participate in God's ongoing narrative. It could be through serving someone in need, offering forgiveness to someone who has wronged you, or stepping out in faith to begin something new. Trust that God will guide you in this process.

Prayer Focus:

- **Pray for Awareness**: Ask God for the eyes to see how He is at work in your life every day, in both the big moments and the small ones. Pray for the ability to recognize His hand guiding you through each chapter.
- **Pray for Courage**: Ask for the courage to embrace the new chapters God is writing in your life. Whether they involve challenges, changes, or new opportunities, pray for the faith to trust in God's plan and follow His lead.
- **Pray for Guidance**: Seek God's wisdom as you move forward in your life's story. Ask for guidance in making decisions that align with His will and contribute to the unfolding of His Kingdom

on earth.

Summary:
Paul's story didn't end with his death, and neither does ours. God is continually writing new chapters in our lives, inviting us to be active participants in His ongoing narrative. Each day offers new opportunities to contribute to God's story, whether through acts of love, service, or simply trusting in His guidance. By recognizing that we are part of a much larger plan, we can approach each moment with purpose and faith, trusting that God is the ultimate author of our lives.

Key Takeaways:

1. **Our Lives Are Part of a Larger Narrative:** Just as Paul's story was part of God's greater plan, so are our lives. God is continually at work, writing new chapters in our lives, and we are invited to participate in His unfolding story.
2. **Challenges Are Part of the Story:** Like Paul, we will face difficulties, but these challenges are not wasted. They are opportunities for growth and transformation, as God shapes us into who He has called us to be.
3. **Each Day Is an Opportunity:** Every day presents a new opportunity to align our lives with God's will and to contribute to His ongoing work in the world.
4. **Trust in God's Authorship:** Our role is not to control or write our own story, but to trust in God's authorship and follow His leading, knowing that His plans are good and purposeful.

By embracing God's ongoing narrative and recognizing our place in His story, we can live with purpose, faith, and a deep sense of trust in His divine plan for our lives.

Chapter Thirteen

Trials and Tribulations
The Cost of Discipleship

Paul's life was defined by trials—imprisonments, beatings, rejection, and threats to his life. Yet, through every hardship, Paul remained unwavering in his commitment to Christ. His life serves as a powerful reminder that following Jesus often comes with a cost, and enduring trials is part of the Christian journey.

The apostle's sufferings are not just historical accounts but timeless examples for every believer. Whether enduring physical persecution, emotional suffering, or spiritual battles, Paul's resilience reflects the core of discipleship: following Christ is a path of surrender, not ease. In a world that prioritizes comfort and personal satisfaction, Paul's life challenges us to examine how much we are willing to endure for the sake of the Gospel.

The Cost of Discipleship: Insights from Bonhoeffer

Dietrich Bonhoeffer, a theologian and martyr during World War II, wrote extensively on the cost of discipleship. In his seminal work *The Cost of Discipleship*, Bonhoeffer emphasizes that grace is costly because it demands a life surrendered to God, and true discipleship means embracing suffering for the sake of Christ. Bonhoeffer's own life, marked by opposition to the Nazi regime and eventual martyrdom, mirrored Paul's willingness to endure for the sake of the Gospel.

Bonhoeffer writes, *"When Christ calls a man, he bids him come and die."* This "death" is both literal and metaphorical: dying to self, pride, and the pursuit of worldly comfort, in order to embrace the life of sacrifice that Christ modeled. Like Paul, Bonhoeffer reminds us that the Christian life is not meant to be easy but is filled with trials that refine us. The cost of discipleship is real, but so is the joy and freedom found in following Jesus.

Modern Application: Embracing Trials Today

In today's world, we may not face the same trials as Paul or Bonhoeffer, but the cost of following Christ remains. Our trials could come in the form of ridicule for standing up for Christian beliefs, societal pressure to compromise our values, or personal struggles that test our faith. We are often asked to make sacrifices—sacrifices of time, comfort, resources, or even relationships—for the sake of living out the Gospel.

Yet, like Paul and Bonhoeffer, we are called to endure these challenges, knowing that God uses them to shape us. The cost of discipleship may involve difficult decisions, loss, or discomfort, but it leads to spiritual maturity and deeper intimacy with Christ.

Reflection Questions

- **What trials are you currently facing that challenge your faith?**
  Are they internal struggles like doubt or external ones such as societal opposition or personal loss?
- **How can you view these challenges as opportunities for spiritual growth?**
  Reflect on how God might be using this season of difficulty to draw you closer to Him and shape your character.
- **In what areas of your life do you resist the cost of discipleship?**
  Is there something you need to surrender to follow Christ more fully, even if it leads to discomfort?

Contemporary Example

GOD'S QUILL CRAFTING YOUR STORY IN DIVINE HARMONY

Consider the story of modern-day Christians facing persecution in hostile regions or enduring hardship in their work or social circles. One example is Pastor Andrew Brunson, an American pastor who was imprisoned in Turkey for his faith in 2016. Despite facing intense pressure to abandon his beliefs, Brunson remained steadfast in his commitment to Christ, even during the darkest days of his imprisonment. His endurance and faith under trial serve as a powerful witness of what it means to embrace the cost of discipleship.

Actionable Steps

- **Identify a trial you are currently facing** and ask God to show you how He is using it to refine your faith. Reflect on how you can use this challenge to deepen your reliance on God and grow spiritually.
- **Reach out to someone who is struggling**, whether emotionally, spiritually, or physically. Offer them support, prayer, and encouragement. By walking alongside others in their trials, you mirror Christ's love.
- **Practice surrendering one area of your life** where you've resisted God's call to sacrifice or endure hardship. Ask God to help you let go of control and trust Him fully, even when it's difficult.

Prayer Focus

- **Pray for strength and perseverance** in the trials you face, asking God to give you the courage to endure and the wisdom to see His hand at work in the midst of suffering.
- **Ask God to help you view trials as opportunities for spiritual growth**, seeking His perspective on the hardships in your life and trusting in His transformative work.
- **Pray for those who are enduring persecution or hardship**

for their faith, that they may remain strong and find encouragement in the knowledge that God is with them in every trial.

Summary and Key Takeaways

- **Key Takeaway 1:** Trials and tribulations are an inherent part of the cost of discipleship. Like Paul, we are called to embrace suffering for the sake of Christ, knowing that it leads to spiritual maturity and a deeper relationship with God.
- **Key Takeaway 2:** God uses our struggles to refine us and draw us closer to Him. When we endure trials with faith, we become more aligned with Christ and His mission.
- **Key Takeaway 3:** The cost of discipleship requires us to let go of worldly comforts and self-preservation, embracing the challenges and sacrifices that come with following Jesus. Through endurance, we experience the power of Christ's grace and transformation.

Final Thoughts

Paul's life and Bonhoeffer's reflections challenge us to reconsider our perspective on trials. Discipleship comes with a cost, but it is a cost worth paying. As followers of Christ, we are invited to view our hardships not as obstacles, but as opportunities to grow in faith, deepen our commitment to the Gospel, and become more like Christ. In the end, the reward is far greater than the cost, for it brings us into closer communion with the One who endured the ultimate suffering on our behalf.

Chapter Fourteen

Epilogue
The Continuing Narrative of Our Lives

Paul's story is not just a testament to transformation but a reminder that God's work in our lives never truly ends. Though Paul's earthly journey concluded, his influence continues to echo through the ages, and God continues to write new chapters in the lives of His people. Similarly, our stories are still unfolding—chapters filled with opportunities for growth, challenges that test our faith, and moments where we are invited to co-author with God the next steps of our journey.

God is the ultimate author, and His plan is far greater than we can imagine. The invitation is open for us to trust Him, to be active participants in this divine narrative. Every act of love, service, and faithfulness is part of this ongoing story. Each day offers us the chance to deepen our faith, embrace our calling, and allow God to continue shaping us for His glory.

The story of Paul encourages us to see our lives through a lens of divine authorship, recognizing that no chapter is wasted, and each page of our story has purpose. Whether you are in a season of joy or trial, God is at work, and He invites you to trust Him with the chapters yet to come.

Modern Application: Living in the Unfolding Story

Today, we are living in God's ongoing narrative, part of a larger, eternal story. Each moment, each decision, and each experience is an opportunity to contribute to that story. Whether through acts of love, service, or simple obedience, we can actively participate in the story God is writing.

Life's twists and turns—both expected and unexpected—are part of the journey. God is constantly at work, shaping us through our experiences and inviting us to trust Him as the ultimate author of our lives. We are called to embrace every chapter, trusting that the ending will always reflect God's perfect purpose.

Reflection Questions

1. **How do you see God writing your story today?**
   Take time to reflect on the moments where God's hand has been evident in your life.
2. **What chapters are still being written in your life?**
   Consider the areas of your life where God may be calling you to trust Him more deeply or to step out in faith.
3. **In what ways can you actively participate in God's ongoing narrative in your life and the lives of others?**
   How can your actions and faith contribute to God's larger plan?

Actionable Steps

- **Reflect on Your Life Story:** Set aside time this week to reflect on how God has been at work in your life. Write down the chapters that have already been written, recognizing the ways God has guided you through challenges and blessings.
- **Pray About the Chapters to Come:** After reflecting on your past, take time to pray about the future chapters of your life. Ask God to guide you and give you the courage to embrace whatever is ahead.
- **Share Your Story:** Find an opportunity to share your story with someone else. Whether through words, a testimony, or a conversation, encourage others by highlighting how God has been at work in your life.

GOD'S QUILL CRAFTING YOUR STORY IN DIVINE HARMONY

Prayer Focus

- **Pray for Awareness:** Ask God to help you recognize how He is working in your life each day, even in the small details. Pray for spiritual eyes to see His hand in every moment.
- **Pray for Courage:** Ask God to give you the courage to embrace the new chapters He is writing in your life, even when they lead you into the unknown or when they require sacrifice. Trust Him with the path ahead.
- **Pray for Faithfulness:** Ask God to help you remain faithful in the role He has given you in His story, using your gifts, talents, and experiences to make a difference for His kingdom.

Summary and Key Takeaways

- **Key Takeaway 1:** Our lives are part of a larger narrative that God is continually writing, and He invites us to participate in His divine plan.
- **Key Takeaway 2:** Every day presents an opportunity to align our actions with God's will, allowing Him to shape us and use us for His greater purpose.
- **Key Takeaway 3:** No chapter in our lives is wasted. Every experience, whether joyful or painful, is part of God's redemptive work, preparing us for what is yet to come.

Final Thoughts

Paul's life reminds us that our stories are always in motion. God is writing a masterpiece with each of our lives, and we are invited to trust Him with every chapter. Whether through triumphs or trials, God's authorship leads us to a deeper purpose and a closer relationship with Him. May we embrace the new chapters with faith and courage, knowing that the One who writes our story is faithful to bring it to completion.

DAVID GRIGGS

Let us continually seek His will, trusting that God is using each of us in His grand narrative to bring about His glory and to fulfill His eternal plan.

Author's Page

David Griggs is a retired pastor who has travelled the world teaching and preaching God 's word in various settings. His travels have taken him to Central and South America, where he taught in local churches and to various mission groups. He has spoken to prisoners in Mozambique, taught graduating students in Sierra Leone and led prayer groups to Mexico. Included within this is his time pastoring and leading local churches.

He is the husband of Esther, the father of three adult children and eight grandchildren. Currently they live in Western New York State.

You can follow him through his website: https://godeeperministries.com and his weekly blogs. His teaching can also be followed on YouTube, Instagram, and Facebook.

Fictional Writings
Hitler's Secret Papers
When Powers Clash
By The Oak Tree Series
The Coming Storm
Flames of Faith
Whispers of Hope
Crime Novel
Brooklyn's Dark Pulse
Various puzzle and coloring books
that can be found on Amazon

Milton Keynes UK
Ingram Content Group UK Ltd.
UKHW021922201124
451474UK00013B/881